Cosmic Office Inc.

Help for You in 7 Speedy Steps

Carol Cary Taylor

"Can I have more than one helper?"

Yes! It's easy to create (imagine, fantasize) assistants with specialized job descriptions. (Chapter 3)

"Why should I read this? I'm already in touch with personal guidance or guides."

Why not? Expand and organize those helpers into your own Cosmic Office Inc. (Chapter 4), and continue to request assistance.

"I want to know about actual helping examples with these helpers."

That's fair. Look for the waves: ~ ~ ~ indicating personal stories throughout Cosmic Office Inc.

Can I share how my own Cosmic Office Inc. assistants have helped me?

Yes! Join others around the world by signing up at www.CosmicOfficeInc.com

Help is always available—all the time!

HOW TO BENEFIT FROM THIS BOOK

(EASY AND FAST)

Every week I hear people say, "But I don't have tim
to do that." For most of my life, I said the same thin;
Now I call on my team of helpers (Cosmic Office Inc
to help me accomplish almost the impossible eve
day.

 Ask yourself:

"Do I need help?"

Yes! Begin at the beginning (Chapter 1), and lea
how to create and meet assistants as fast as you c:
imagine them!

"Do I need more time?"

Yes! Who doesn't? There may only be 24 hours ir
day, but your time can be enhanced and made m(
productive with helpers that only work for you.

 "Do I believe there's more to life than meets the ey(

Yes...or maybe. Go directly to types of helpers that y
create—for yourself—and start working with y(
personalized and unique office staff. (Chapter 2)

CONTENTS

How to Benefit from this book

"If one is lucky, a solitary fantasy can totally transform one million realities."

-- Maya Angelou

1 CONNECT WITH PERSONAL ASSISTANCE

Believe it's possible
Cosmic Office Inc. is born

Could you use help? What if personal staff members were immediately accessible and only had your best interests at heart? Sounds too good (or outrageous) to be true? Help is available, but... there's a catch. Anyone who believes and trusts that support ("gut feelings," intuition, inspiration, guidance) is constantly available while making an effort (doing the work) will be rewarded.

In other words, an imagined staff of assistants is a cooperative, give and take collaboration between personally-imagined helpers and their manager (you). And, since those helpers are blended figments of your imagination, formed through your personal mindset with your personality quirks and your values, the information and outcomes will be arriving already personalized. Why? Because you are the creator, administrator, and manager of your own staff ("Cosmic Office Inc.").

Concepts and beliefs

Possibilities are endless! Welcome to invisible guidance that could be an angelic being, God, a Spirit Guide, the Divine, the "Force," etc. What do you believe possible? Consider that an energy source connecting everything in the cosmos may also provide unlimited assistance to anyone living and working on earth. For example, have you ever been inexplicably slowed by traffic or red lights only to discover that the delay time prevented your involvement in an accident? While passing the scene of wreckage and flashing lights of emergency vehicles, did you send blessings or a prayer to the victims as well as thanks to your "guardian angels?"

Since the beginning of time, instances of extraordinary, unbelievable luck or good fortune have been recorded and illustrated in art and literature. Examples abound in which people happen to be at the right (or wrong) place at the right (or wrong) time in the right (or wrong) circumstances. Could it be destiny? Or could it be some type of divine intervention? And could that intervention possibly be a connection with guidance or nonphysical spirit? Various traditions and writings have described assistance as originating with the Divine, or angels, or guides, or answered prayers, or the unknown.

A wide variety of positive experiences (many included in this book), led me to believe in divine or unexplainable possibilities and responses. I also sense that the cosmic, or universal, energy of personalized help is an integral piece of my total being. That is, individual guides (which I imagine as a personal staff) have been with me forever. I'm not sure whether they are angels, guides, or divine assistance of some kind, but I know that I have been helped and even protected all through my life—maybe even before birth!

A few hours before my early morning birth, my father and aunt spent most of the day and evening shoveling snow. They were trying to keep up with the accumulation in the driveway so my mother could be driven to the hospital in time for her first baby's arrival. The hospital was only twelve miles away, but the ride on unlighted, unplowed, snowy roads must have been treacherous. Fortunately, my parents were the proud owners of a Jeep® and in a few hours I arrived healthy and apparently happy at the hospital.

Fast-forwarding to today—is it a coincidence that I safely drive thousands of miles each year, and that my first car was a Jeep? Who can say?

In written history

Have you ever felt the presence of help or protection at any time in your life? I believe there are powers beyond our imagination and physical human limits (regardless of their otherworldly names or titles) and that assistance is always available. Similar thoughts have been recorded through the ages—from ancient and biblical times to modern recollections and the opinions of consciousness explorers.

A belief that "Divine Force" was an integral part of everything in Ancient Mesopotamia meant that the natural and supernatural were the same; with an otherworldly anticipation that humankind (as "the gods' co-workers") would fulfill its missions on earth.

Divine assistance is mentioned throughout the *Bible* in the New Testament. Paul wrote: "We are God's fellow-workers; and you are God's garden."[1] In the Old Testament are the words: "For he has charged his angels to guard you wherever you go, to lift you on their hands for fear you should strike your foot against a stone."[2]

Reports of divine assistance are also mentioned in modern times. Author John Randolph Price writes of sightings and angelic friend and guide connections.[3]

Do you suppose that angelic or spiritual beings are real? If so, you're not alone! According to a 2011 Associated Press-GfK poll of American adults, 77% believe so.[4] Rosalind McKnight was one of the 77%. She was often in contact with a radiant "Spirit friend" who provided guidance and information: "Spirit is in a no-time existence, and multitasking is one of the angels' prime talents. They can perform a thousand tasks at once if necessary because in no-time everything is possible. Life on the Earth plane is linear, but in the spirit world it is all-encompassing. The angels exist in the spirit world but are constantly in tune with your spirit. Any time you call or pray for help and guidance, they are instantly aware, and are with you to protect and guide you."[5]

This spiritual power beyond what can be considered possible on earth may be referred to as prayer, divine guidance, helpers, God, or other names based on individual religious or philosophical beliefs.

As a child, did you have an imaginary friend? If so, you may have considered any connections with that friend as normal, interactive parts of your life. Most adults have forgotten those special connections as childhood beliefs are modified, changed, and perhaps obliterated by harsh experiences, adult judgments, and other points of view.

Reason and intuition

Don't believe? No problem! History and literature are full of suggestions on how to connect with the guidance of inner, intuitive dimensions that are perceived as exclusive to each person's identity. Consider that "Know thyself" came from Ancient

Greece. In modern times, Ralph Waldo Emerson has stated in his "Self Reliance" essay: "A man should learn to detect and watch that gleam of light which flashes across the mind from within, more than the lustre of the firmament of bards and sages."[6]

Connections with the unseen are described in various philosophies and through personal, often originally skeptical, assumptions—particularly in exploring and recording information of otherworldly realms. Trained scientist and doctor Eben Alexander conceptualizes (with an in-the-moment sense) a grand and unlimited universe[7] with an omnipresent, unconditionally loving God with whom we are all divinely connected "...as One..."[8]

What's the source of unseen or divine contact and information? Who really knows? I think any person's idea may differ from another's through personal experiences, beliefs, and perceptions—such as sensing a "feeling" or "knowing it in my bones."

Rosalind McKnight, as an early explorer with Robert Monroe, contributed to his research in accessing discrete levels of consciousness. She has documented her meetings with unseen helpers and asked many questions, including "...how do spirit guides and guardian angels get the attention of the ones they are assigned to who aren't sensitive to their presence?" The answer as it came to her: "Your 'gut feeling' and intuition are two important ways that your helpers can get your attention. Also, when you get that 'knowing' feeling, you should always heed it. It is very hard for spiritual helpers to work with humans that live so much through their heads and ignore their heart levels."[9]

Getting your attention

How could an invisible source of guidance get your attention? There are a variety of ways—all depending on the person at the receiving end (you). In addition to "hunches," or "gut feelings," information can arrive unconsciously during a relaxed, possibly familiar and repetitive motion (taking a shower), during times of personally-evoked meditation or prayer,[10] through dream symbology (if the sleeper isn't too impatient and tired to notice), and a variety of the senses.[11]

Do you learn easiest by listening? If so, pay attention to sounds in nature, chance conversations, and song lyrics. During an episode of the "Ally McBeal" television series, the lead character (Ally) hears a certain ("favorite") tune that instantly creates a personal moment of joyful song and dance.[12] Most of us have at least one favorite song or bit of music that somehow changes our mood and inspires us to keep going with new energy.

Recently, this "sound synchronicity" arrived during a mental funk of my own. I was feeling uninspired and unappreciated, and then heard the perfect song (with the perfect, personally-directed lyrics) at the perfect time. Hearing it immediately changed my mood and focus.

For visual learners, appearances can be especially helpful, particularly if in a positive frame of mind. Often, visible "clutter" has to be edited out of a typical perception picture with intention and practice. Many of us notice clues and information visually and instinctively take notice when startled by something seen "out of the corner of my eye."

Occasionally, a certain smell or scent will help make a connection to the treasures and memory of the unconscious; but in my attention-getting experiences, sometimes it's the message and sometimes it's how the message (information) is presented that adds to any understandings.

Regardless of how information is personally presented, people requesting and open to assistance tend to immediately know—without a shadow of a doubt—that the information is so personally relevant and special that it can only be meant for them, and them alone.

Tuning in, waiting for answers

Some individuals have daily experiences as they connect with forms of help or guidance that are in agreement with the authors of *Companions in Spirit* (Laeh Maggie Garfield and Jack Grant). They write that personal helpers even realize (maybe before you do!) that a request has been made verbally or mentally. The answer or information asked for is made obvious—maybe so obvious that it's impossible to avoid bumping into it.

Rosalind McKnight, in frequent communication with her spirit guide, learned that there is a team for each person on earth and sometimes the team members/guides have to get our attention. A book might fall off a shelf that "happens" to have the perfect information, for example. As the guide explains, "That's why you have guides. God covers all the bases. If you need help, ask—and you'll definitely get an answer."[13]

According to Esther Hicks and her information from "Abraham" ("teachers of teachers"): "Every being who is in physical form at this time is currently receiving communication from another dimension, from an inner dimension, from their Inner Being."[14]

The realization that help is available was comfortable and easy to grasp. The appreciation of help I could also easily understand. It was trusting in these guides/parts of self that was difficult. Did I have the ability to ask someone imagined out of thin air for help? And would the invisible helpers be dependable and assist me in producing important results? Being curious, I sent requests through my imagination (such as "Remember this!" or "Don't forget ____"), with the hope that any results would be helpful, but not absolutely essential.

What happened next was astounding, with results so personally valuable and extraordinary that I began to believe and rely not only in assistants I couldn't see, but in assistance I could! It was a life-changing experience of learning and trusting. After receiving almost immediate help and answers that came to me at the perfect time, I became even more confident and convinced that I could widen my horizons. I imagined specific helpers and asked for even more assistance, and the responses continued to amaze. Soon I had no doubt about the power of my guides/helpers, the infinite possibilities of what isn't always obvious, and myself.

Creating Cosmic Office Inc.

Have you ever received a mental "uh oh!" in your life? The type of intuitive reminders making one anxiously wonder: "Did I leave the _____ on?" "Did I remember to _____ before I left the house?" I recognize these "prompts" as intuitive nudges that help me to pay attention. Once, in the middle of the night, I woke up—fearful of forgetting something important for the next day of work. Since I was already awake, I should have written myself a reminder note. Did I do that? No. I was comfortable and cozy and thought I would probably fall back asleep and somehow remember that critical information. Instead, I worried for hours about what might be forgotten. Then the wake up alarm rang, and a restless night of tossing and turning became a day of unfocused fatigue.

Has this ever happened to you?

Cosmic Office Inc. was born of necessity—for sleep! The next time I was awakened with a sudden "Remember _____!" alert, I created a personal memory helper to not only help me remember, but to provide the information to me as needed. This helper soon became a reliable special assistant, so when awakened with a "must not forget" thought, I woke up, consciously turned over the task of remembering to my memory assistant, and easily fell back asleep— confident that a reminder would come along when I could take care of it in the daytime. Dependable and often extraordinary answers resulted, and I learned to rely on my helper more and more—and to appreciate the assistant and the assistance.

Where does this helper hang out? Maybe in my imagination. And since I believe that imagination is unlimited, I guessed that this helper was somehow part of my own energy. It seemed to be near, yet invisible; and not necessarily physical. I gave this helper a name so when asking for specific assistance, I mentally called on a certain assistant. It felt like a real partnership, with each of us adding what we could to get a job done. When we finished, I somehow knew whom to thank.

Then, since I needed a lot of help, I decided to "hire" more helpers, give them names, and ask for more and more support. Soon the number of personal assistants grew larger, and presto! Somewhere in the cosmos I had a staff! A staff much larger than anything in my working life! So much larger, in fact, that I had to organize these newly created helpers into a kind of personal office to keep track of all of them.

Suddenly, the Cosmic Office—an energetic and fantastic consulting team with only my best interests at heart—was born! Creating this staff, or office, has been an incredible learning experience. There's a clearer understanding of unlimited potential, what may be possible, and 24/7 assistance.

Your personal staff at work

Cosmic Office Inc. is an imagined staff for personalized help beyond what can be humanly and physically accomplished on earth.

Every month I drive 600-plus miles on congested Interstate highways with frequent accidents, back ups, and delays. I "do the work" by maintaining the vehicle, filling it with gas, and remaining calm and responsible for my driving—all the while realizing that events beyond my control could happen at any time. The route is mapped, I've packed, and have cash and credit cards. Then, I drive safely and stay alert. These details are obviously necessary and can be accomplished by anyone.

But what about surprises (traffic jams, roadwork, unexpected weather events, accidents or other delays) that no one can predict?

I turn over any "surprises" of traffic, safety, and even highway conditions to my unseen staff. How? I imagined a road condition manager, a traffic controller, a car maintenance expert, and a route director. Now, while I do the driving, these helpers are asked to provide the perfect driving experience (even if that requires extra prayer and patience with detours and delays).

~ ~ ~

I was picking up a friend flying into town, but missed the airline location signs, and had to exit and re-enter the airport as my friend anxiously waited for me curbside. On the second try (and fifteen minutes later), she was located and away we went. In less than half an hour, however, I slowed down at a "slippery when wet" sign and narrowly avoided being hit by two cars skidding across the road and into a ditch. The drivers may have braked too late and started sliding out of control. Who knows? They were shaken but unharmed (their vehicles weren't), and my friend was relieved that we had steered clear of any accident.

My immediate thought was gratitude—to my travel staff—for helping with the driving circumstances and perfect timing. What if I had noticed the airline gate location and found my friend earlier? What if I had been speeding and trying to make up for the lost time? It's difficult to say, but I'm convinced that my helpers were on the job; and if not them, maybe other assistance or guidance? Every moment of the day has the potential for the unexpected, perhaps "unexplained," event or set of circumstances to unfold.

In other words, assigning travel tasks to invisible assistants of my own creation and belief is no excuse for ignoring important responsibilities (following all the traffic laws, paying attention, keeping the car maintained). Suggestions coming from intuition may mean taking one route over another or driving more slowly, but safe arrivals for me happen by being aware, patient, trusting, and appreciative of invisible, yet always present, support.

Asking for help

How should I ask? Many authors who depend on personal helpers know from experience that requests should be made with genuine sincerity and desire. They may also believe that anything of value to a life experience will take place (whether or not it seems obvious), and that it's best not to have any preconceived notion of how (or when) the reply will arrive.

Start by focusing, asking yourself what would be helpful, and trying not to be overwhelmed by the unlimited variety of possibilities. Begin with something modest or small-scale, learning to reconnect with your own imagination and a specific helper.

If possible, detach from any fear of disappointment. Why be afraid? Young children, until told differently, ask Santa Claus for all kinds of stuff! And even if they don't get everything on their lists, they will keep asking. This topic is quoted all through recorded history. In the *Bible*: "Ask, and you will receive; seek, and you will find; knock, and the door will be opened. For everyone who asks receives, he who seeks finds, and to him who knocks, the door will be opened."[15]

Do you entertain the possibility that assistance is yours for the asking? Considering such a possibility, existence, or potential of personal help is an introductory step in creating your own fantasy helpers.

~ ~ ~

Before creating my personal Cosmic Office staff with energy and in faith, I frequently asked people for help; but I must have been doing something wrong. Usually I received no support, nothing. Each discouraging let down added to my disillusionment and the idea that help wasn't available to me (and why not? I'm a good and worthy person!). Maybe I have to be very specific and to guess the right time to ask for someone's help (when they aren't in the middle of something and I have their complete attention). Or maybe I'm asking the wrong people, or maybe I'm not using the best words or phrases, or at some deeper, been-hurt-and-disappointed-before level, maybe I'm not expecting to receive assistance—therefore sabotaging the outcome. Or, maybe down deep, I'm embarrassed to admit that I can't do everything myself. Whew!

Never afraid to ask, Rosalind McKnight asked her guide: "Is there always someone out there listening to us, watching us, waiting to help?" and her guide replied, "'As you think, your thought is connected to the pure mind of God.' So when you ask for help, you will receive help. That is a universal principle. 'Ask and you will receive.'"[16]

Will you receive assistance? Since you have created your own attentive and loyal helpers ready with personalized assistance for you at any time...yes! Plus, the guidance is coming from your imagination, so there isn't any personal judging, choosing "best" timeframes, or serious disappointment. Even so, answers or assistance may arrive in unusual forms. Pay attention by tuning into dreams ("Dreams say what they mean, but they don't say it in daytime language"- Gail Godwin),[17] "out of the corner of my eye" perceptions, hunches, prayers, meditations, and intuitional "zaps" of realization.

Musician/composer Quincy Jones in the book *Positive Energy*, mentions his connection with a version of this intuitive, "knowing" feeling. After asking his subconscious helpers for assistance before going to sleep, he awakens with a variety of ideas (plus music) that he promptly writes down. He and I and many others who rely on divine help agree that the universe holds all the information we would want to know.[18] We merely have to ask, pause, and listen.

Also recognize and respect your presence on earth (in a profound, heart-based way) "...and that you deserve all the assistance that spiritual and earthly beings can extend."[19]

Ask for what?

Is anything possible? It depends on each person's beliefs. Walt Disney famously said, "If you can dream it, you can do it."[20]

Historical writings provide amazing examples of positive, anything is possible, events and gifts arriving through connections with personal belief. But what will we ask for? I believe we're all on earth to learn and grow through exploring and wondering, so ask away! Ask for help even if you don't know your heart's desire and what might be helpful. Still doubtful or unsure? Ask that "the perfect" information or assistance come to your attention—at the perfect time for perfect positive benefit. And then pay attention and expect to receive.

Huh?

What if the answer makes no sense? Many people wonder, "What does _____ mean?" Ask about a meaning or significance that isn't immediately understood. It's okay! You're doing the asking, for your benefit, so wondering about possible answers is part of the learning process. When in doubt, ask the same question over and over until the answer arrives, since helpers are very patient. I believe that continuing to engage with the power and energy of our intuitions creates the basis for confidence and extraordinary personal growth.

Now, with a few basic steps, you can invent your own "office," a personalized creation of your own ingenuity. You may also begin to connect regularly with invisible help. As imagined helpers are organized into a personal staff, it may also be easier to manage what has been described as coincidence, connection, synchronicity, chance, guidance, luck, blessings, intuition, or answers to prayer.

Consider that this personal group of working helpers is available to assist and enrich your life. Are you interested in connecting with the power of your imagination? Do you believe that a fantastic version of unlimited possibility, power, desire, direction, and positive energy in a helping team is available?

Are you inspired to manage your destiny? Create your own Cosmic Office Inc. now—in 7 Speedy Steps!

"Light is the task when many share the toil."

-- Homer

2 GET TO KNOW YOUR "COSMIC COMMITTEE"

Create a personal helping staff in 7 Speedy Steps

What types of help do you need every day? What tasks or chores are especially difficult? Now, imagine a few helpers, guides, assistants, co-workers, or cosmic helpers to call upon on a daily basis or "as needed." If you like to be involved in micro-managing everything or if your life is really complicated, a full staff and even an office manager can be invented for the ultimate "Cosmic Office Inc."

Creating unlimited staff members with titles or names can easily be achieved by visioning and believing anything is possible. Focus on a task (not an outcome) that requires more time, energy, or even expertise than you might have. Keep it simple and begin with a single task at a time. With practice and positive experiences, add to your staff and assign specific assignments—all the while being aware of "incoming" results and answers. Be alert to possible clues or signs of staff support as results and answers come into your awareness—day or night.

7 Speedy Steps to take

1. Believe that help is yours for the asking.
2. Trust that each helper has your best interests at heart.

3. Decide to ask for help.

4. Intentionally imagine or invent a helper.

5. Act or "do the work" necessary.

6. Be aware of possible clues or signs of staff support.

7. Appreciate every step in the process.

7 Steps in detail

Cosmic Office is the opportunity to meet and greet individual helpers, who (as integral parts of your own self/imagination) are loyal, trustworthy, and always available. It's a personal choice—which helpers, and what kind of help, would be welcome? Since the possibilities (and your needs) can be overwhelming, begin with one or two helpers, focus on what assistance would be helpful, and keep it simple.

1. Believe that anything is possible and that help is available, and continue...

2. Trust that the perfect personal information will arrive in the perfect manner at the perfect time. Relax during each of the steps, removing yourself from any pre-conceived ideas of how, when, and what kind of assistance may occur.

3. Decide what help would be useful and best for your life and lifestyle. Are you a parent, an entrepreneur, an employee, an artist? What daily or weekly tasks require more expertise, time, or even enthusiasm than you can possibly provide? What help would be helpful? Many of us could benefit with

assistance in remembering, traveling, relaxing, organizing, creating, sleeping, confidence-building, entertaining, or almost anything. Don't know what's needed? No problem! Get calm and quiet and sincerely ask: "What would best assist me?"

4. Intentionally create the perfect staff member for a task, as if hiring for an organization (and you are that organization) and assign responsibilities. Since the creating of staff members and their titles or names is limited only by imagination, and imagination is unlimited, personalize and have fun with the process. What terms seem right to you: Manager? Consultant? Helper? Guidance? Friend? Or a special nickname? I add a gender non-specific "Pal" to the name/describer of each of my helpers. In other words, the staff member responsible for helping me recapture what's been forgotten is "Memo Pal." You may prefer "Memory Guy" or "Memo Gal" or "Memo Friend." Or not. Select a title that's personal, comfortable to say, and easy to remember—anything that differentiates your helper from the other Cosmic Office staff and allows for easy and effortless contact.

5. Take responsibility for actions that may be required and necessary to receive information or to reach a goal. Working with your "office," or staff, is a cooperative two-way street.[21] In addition to believing in possibility, creating and relying on staff, and asking for help, actually doing the work necessary is critical to any success. This action step is your solid contribution while the invisible assistance—whatever that may be—is occurring in the cosmos. Depending on the goal, your responsibility during this helping

process could include personally deciding what to do, making telephone calls, looking for job openings in a variety of media, writing and answering emails, filling out forms, searching the Internet, taking classes, driving safely with recommended car maintenance, and anything else involved with the project or assignment.

6. Be aware, pay attention, and tune into your sixth sense (intuition) while the assistance is ongoing. This helping process could take a while, be invisible, and appear when least expected. What clues are coming to you from others, from your physical senses, from "gut feelings" or nudges? Which of these will you judge best for the situation? See, smell, touch, listen, taste, open your brain, reconnect with the natural world, put the mobile device aside, and link with your own "there's only one of me" authenticity.

7. Appreciate and thank. No task, assistance, or action is too small to ever be taken for granted. Your staff of helpers, created personally by yourself, ultimately has your best, most outstanding, interests and goals[22] going on behind the scenes. When a (previously thought impossible) goal is reached or when obvious answers and amazing connections are occurring, saying thanks is easy. But even the tiniest, least noticeable, accomplishments require "an attitude of gratitude."[23] Depending on when the "Ah-ha!" moment of receiving happens, I am always sincerely grateful and will say a silent or audible "thank you" to my Cosmic Office helper.

Working with your staff

There are major differences between your "virtual," or imagined group of assistants and human employees or co-workers. Since you created your staff members, they provide individual assistance just for you, at your request. Plus, your Cosmic Office of helpers exists within your unlimited imagination. Answers or services or even the number of "employees" in the organization known as you is unlimited. They go wherever you go! Plus, work hours are irrelevant in this insightful "no-time" realm, so help is available 24 hours a day—every day!

Once a few basic helping "partners" have been named, realize that you have met, made contact with, and created a trustworthy staff solely for yourself—with your own energy—originating from your own beliefs. Various writers (including Shakti Gawain) refer to this helper type as "...a higher part of yourself, which can come to you in many different forms..."[24]

~ ~ ~

I was looking for a job and called on my trustworthy "Hiring Pal" to assist—knowing and believing from experience that an ideal position would turn up at the perfect time. All I had to do was relax, pay attention, and act on any incoming clues and directions. The car had to be inspected that month, so I arrived at the garage early—only to learn there was a one hour wait. What to do? Stay in the reception area with someone who was coughing and sniffling, or leave? I headed out for coffee, but the first two places weren't open yet. The third location was open with friendly servers, indoor seating and newspapers.

With no place to go for an hour, I started to relax by sitting down with a cup of coffee to read the local paper. It was almost time to walk back to the garage when I noticed a hard-to-miss quarter-page ad in the classified section. It advertised the perfect job at the perfect place, with perfect hours, with qualifications that perfectly matched mine, and (almost) perfect pay! Wow! In that moment, I felt as if a gift had arrived...just for me! On the walk back to the garage, I mentally composed a cover letter, and by afternoon had sent off the required transcripts, recommendation letters, and application form. Three days later, I was called for an interview, and in two more days I started working at a job which was...perfect.

This account is a true and perhaps astonishing example of a Cosmic Office staff providing assistance. Although possibilities are unlimited, the actual job didn't just fall from the sky or land in my lap. In other words, I believed and trusted (from past experiences) that assistance would arrive. I decided to ask for help—intentionally assigning "Hiring Pal" for the task, and I acted by choosing to avoid the waiting room, walking until I found coffee, and buying the newspaper. I read the paper (even the ads) with awareness, carefully followed directions, and mailed the entire application package—all the while appreciating the gift of the information.

After the paperwork had been sent, the outcome was out of my control and I knew it was okay to relax and let go of any ego or attachment as much as possible (also mentioned in Deepak Chopra's *The Seven Spiritual Laws of Success*).[25]

Each assistant, as well as its assistance, must be acknowledged with appreciation. During the job search, I sincerely thanked all of the helping energies I had called on (Hiring Pal, Application Pal, Interview Pal, Perfect Coworker Pal); but there may have been more. Who knows? When in doubt, try to visualize a self-created bubble of blissful gratitude surrounding yourself, helpers, and the entire procedure. Since staff is created from my own imagination, I can easily give everyone a day off and even dream up occasions for celebration—complete with champagne. And I never forget to schedule office parties on holidays!

For your Cosmic Office success, thanking and being grateful may seem to be the easiest of the seven steps—certainly after being on the receiving end of fantastic assistance—but it's important.

After months or years, help may become automatic and natural, but never underestimate positive power or your own potential. Make a daily habit of being present with your self and grateful for all gifts beginning with physical senses, the invisible, and nature (fresh air, sunshine, water). A constant attitude of appreciation is an important part of each step, as it seems to promote even more of a connection not only with each helper, but with your true, authentic self or identity.

Still doubtful?

You may realize that your own intention has created positions and titles of dependable Cosmic Office associates. But you may not yet believe that anything is possible. This human, "prove it" feeling is natural, but probably temporary (at least until results come your way). I have learned this: as long as I continue to trust in perfect outcomes, do any work that seems necessary for the task, and don't worry about the outcome, help is taking place behind the scenes.

Maybe "The Little Prince" had the idea when he said, "Anything essential is invisible to the eyes."[26] Certainly, every obvious conclusion with fantastical results feels like another example of contact and connection with my loyal helpers. By trusting, believing, asking, and acting, more of the unlimited potential beyond physical, touchable, contact is possible.

To reach outcomes and goals, this personal thought and deliberate action in every step of Cosmic Office staff creating is critical. According to Napoleon Hill, an acknowledged personal-success expert, "First comes the thought; then, organization of that thought into ideas and plans; then transformation of those plans into reality. The beginning, as you will observe, is in your imagination."[27] Within the framework of your personal staff, first there's the choice to believe and trust that help is available; then the decision and intention to ask for assistance; then a thoughtful commitment to act, be aware, and appreciate—all in a positive, appreciative frame of mind and action.

Since the aim is one of positive, helpful outcomes, I recommend creating helpers proactively with the best of intentions. Creating helpers with the task to not do something puts attention on what isn't wanted, and why do that?

Although we, as human beings, have free will and choice, being upbeat and looking at a glass half full has a powerful effect on anyone's life situation.

Examples of providing thoughts (positive or negative) that form thoughtful outcomes are found throughout history. The Buddha is credited with: "We are shaped by our thoughts; we become what we think." The phrase "like attracts like" also occurs in various traditions and is the basis for the Law of Attraction. Popular author Louise Hay writes that anyone's future is created by the power of words, thoughts, and thinking that "...create our experiences."[28]

Help arrives

How does the assistance show up in our lives? Help may arrive through a strong personal emotion, voice, action, or from a spiritual presence. Who knows? At this point in my life, I choose to extend my imagination beyond boundaries that far surpass the confining and restrictive beliefs of my youth— agreeing with Robert Monroe who writes: "The greatest illusion is that mankind has limitations."[29] In addition to the act of thinking, perhaps the 'thoughts as actual things' idea holds some clues.

In 1796, patriot Thomas Paine wrote "...there are two distinct classes of what are called Thoughts: those that we produce in ourselves by reflection and the act of thinking, and those that bolt into the mind of their own accord. I have always made it a rule to treat these voluntary visitors with civility, taking care to examine, as well as I was able, if they were worth entertaining; and it is from them I have acquired almost all the knowledge that I have."[30]

It could be that those "voluntary visitors" represent inspiration which is defined as "spirit; a breathing of life into."[31]

Many of us have received ideas that seem to "...bolt into the mind of their own accord." Since your office is positively created in your imagination, there is no need to limit the possibilities, no need to place any restrictions, and no need to impose personal expectations of outcomes ("Do it only my way"). Any staff request could be brief and urgent ("Please locate the perfect parking space"), something immediate and complex (getting hired), or even a request for eventual results (writing a book). Consider what would be helpful, request assistance, relax, do what's necessary, and trust that the staff members are working—with your personal support and cooperation—for perfect results.

Learn to recognize when help arrives or when staff aid may have intervened. Being open to opportunities and assistance or occurrences that may be beyond your wildest expectations is also important. Every moment of the day has the potential for the unexpected, perhaps "unexplained" event or set of circumstances to unfold. Incoming information may grab your attention and be apparent and obvious that it is exclusively and only for you.

Assistance, including information, is available for the asking—particularly for anyone who trusts and enthusiastically works with their Cosmic Office staff on a regular basis. It doesn't matter who you are or where you live. With daily contact, intuition can expand and become an even more valuable personal asset.

~ ~ ~

As an adult, I have been trying to overcome a childhood fear of snakes, but a member of my Cosmic Office staff can apparently sense my ongoing anxiety because I'm frequently "reminded" that the creatures have a place in the natural ecosystem. Here is one example: while walking in my garden and preoccupied with wondering which water lilies were blooming, a reflex action brought me to a screeching halt. The glistening color of a freshly-shed copperhead snakeskin was immediately ahead (and in the exact location of my next step). Yikes! With a sudden and surprised intake of breath, I immediately had the thought: "Go no further!" It was clear and strong and there wasn't a doubt in my mind that I was being warned. Without the snakeskin sign or "clue," I may have mindlessly continued, getting too close to the unstable, rocky edge and a sheer drop. Who knows for certain what may have happened? But I am absolutely sure that somehow I had received help just in time. I sent thanks to a helper (possibly a guardian angel?) and appreciation for the snake's molted warning.

You are the president, the supervisor, the star; and in charge of your life experience. Therefore, it's up to you to imagine your own Cosmic Office with the 7 Speedy Steps: believe, trust, decide, intend, act, be aware, appreciate. Once created and in place, working with your helpers regularly will establish unlimited connections of assistance.

What does the Cosmic Office help you accomplish? That would depend on what you believe can be requested, how often you assign tasks of projects to staff, how long the physical work takes, and how you recognize any and all benefits.

Becoming familiar with your assistants doesn't take much time, and after reading this book, you can immediately create your own office with fantasy workers.

~ ~ ~

After a recent presentation on energy modalities, there was time remaining and I asked the group if anyone would be interested in hearing about my Cosmic Office idea. Receiving a positive, though curious ("What?") response, I segued into a speedy, unrehearsed explanation that only half of the audience seemed to grasp. The other half of the audience, however, easily connected with the very basic instruction and went on to create and name helpers, offices, staffs, and to use them in a variety of situations. I received this email later:

"Hi Dear Carol,

Thank you for your knowledgeable and interesting presentation in July. I did really enjoy it as well as you being the presenter.

As you remember my sister and niece were at that meeting also. My niece is fluent in English but I still questioned her as to how much she really did understand. The Chinese medicine info she understood perfectly but the "virtual office" idea was a little beyond her grasp. I tried to explain it further but thought the best way is to use it so..... we were leaving the shore and driving to NYC for their last week in the states before returning to Italy. I told her we are asking our driving committee to help us with this trip.

First let's ask the protection task force to protect us during the trip up north. Then the traffic coordinator to help us avoid traffic jams and accidents. We left on a Sunday with all the others returning from their vacations especially driving on the NJ turnpike. All went fine and even when we stopped at the rest/snack places we found very close spots to the entrances. We made great time considering the day, time and summer season.

After going through the Lincoln tunnel and arriving in NYC I said now we need to start speaking to the parking spot committee as it is always difficult to find a spot, but it is especially difficult on Sunday afternoon when all the "good spots" (alternate side of the street for Monday are already parked in, NYC mentality) are even harder to find. Driving uptown on 10th Ave. every light turned green just as we approached it so we drove uptown without stopping for one single light. Now I have had this happen to me on occasion but usually at 2 or 3 AM in the morning with practically no traffic, never during the day with other traffic beside me.

Wait it gets better. We now travel across town to the East side nearing my Aunt's apartment. I now announce it was time to call in our parking helpers for the best spot possible. 2 blocks away we find a spot and my niece points to it. I decided that we would not park there, but pull into my Aunt's apartment driveway and ask the doormen to help us with all our stuff and after we unload I would look for a spot. At my Aunt's there are already 2 other cars in the driveway unloading so I changed my mind and said, "Plan B, we will get a spot and make 2 or 3 trips with all our stuff." So driving down the block at two or three nothing was available, no parking and I began to think what a mistake I made not to take that first spot. I even said, "Oh boy I really blew it." My sister told me to go around and up the same route when we started looking. I thought no way will the spot still be there at least 10 minutes later. We drove down and around that same block and there it was, the SAME spot. Unbelievable!!!! and yes we parked and did not have to worry about Monday parking either. Any person in NYC I told this story to could not believe it. My niece would just tell them that "Aunt N." has a whole committee with her when she travels and they can really help her.

Now before she is leaving for Italy, I'm home in VA and she calls to say good-bye etc. and tells me, "don't worry I have called in my committee to be there at JFK so they will help Mom and I with the luggage and all our travels." Their trip was uneventful, no problems, but the cherry on the cake was when they arrived in Pisa, their luggage was already out waiting for them to pick up!!! What a great lesson you taught that day at B's house.

Hope you are doing well and your book is moving along as it should be with your virtual office workers' help.

Be well. Many blessings,
N"

If "N" could create her own personally-named ("committee") version of Cosmic Office with imagined staff members (driving committee, protection task force, traffic coordinator, parking spot committee) one month after hearing a short 15-minute description, imagine what you can do with more time and all of the suggestions in the next chapter!

3 JOB DESCRIPTIONS OF HELPERS

Titles and Roles for Assistants

What help do you need during a typical day? It's possible to have a personal core team of helpers, guides, co-workers, cosmic helpers, specialists, angels on duty, or others (fill in your preferred name) for a variety of assignments. Or, create a staff for every area of your life (personal, educational, professional, recreational).

Before creating any assistants, recognize yourself as Chief Executive Officer (CEO) of the organization known as You—responsible for leading, managing, and directing. As this decision-making, "buck stops here" authority figure, your free choice and thinking are always in play. A CEO (you) is in charge—from daily work activity to maintaining clear and sincere connections with the staff of your own personally-imagined office in the invisible energy of the encompassing cosmos.

Ready to create your Cosmic Office Inc. staff now? Start with Step One and continue through all 7 Speedy Steps while asking yourself: "What would best serve my personal situation or lifestyle?" Make a list, or roster, with the name of each fantasy helper you have imagined (the list can always be changed easily and quickly).

The "7 Speedy Steps" (more details in Chapter 2)

1. Believe that help is yours for the asking.
2. Trust that each helper has your best interests at

heart.

3. Decide to ask for help.
4. Intentionally imagine or invent a helper.
5. Act or "do the work" necessary.
6. Be aware of possible clues or signs of staff support.
7. Appreciate every step in the process.

Basic assistants to add or subtract

Car Maintenance Pal - can provide reminders regarding oil changes, tire rotations, tune-ups, state inspections, etc.

Make a mental note of when maintenance should happen and ask for assistance in remembering to make (and keep) appointments. I also request help in locating (getting recommendations for) the best repair people.

Clearing Pal - clears mental clutter and distractions.

Not feeling in control due to urgent demands and (possibly unnecessary) details? Ask for help in unloading personal stress and stressors and begin to relax. It's also helpful to put distance between yourself and the electricity in buildings, mobile devices, WiFi, and computers by getting to a park and walking on earth (not concrete) amid trees and nature.

Coach - also known as the "Nudger."
Provides an extra push or gentle reminder to help get past procrastination blocks.

~ ~ ~

I like to dawdle and daydream. It's easy and feels

better than actually getting something done until I have to. Many times, my parents had to literally bribe me to do something ("I'll pay for this _____if you _____"). Now that I'm older and can imagine the potential for positive actions, this staff member stays very busy—especially when I'm trying to put off the inevitable consequences of delay or inaction. Hours and days can vanish if I don't ask Coach for motivation with any chore demanding my attention. At this exact moment (with cosmic help), I'm sitting at the computer rather than doing something (anything) that's more fun.

Commute Pal - can manage your commuting process.

While you do the traveling and regularly turn over anything beyond your control (traffic conditions, traffic lights, mass-transit seating and delays) to this staff member, commuting can become less stressful. Create an imaginary car pool by adding your Cosmic Office Parking, Travel, and Time Efficiency pals.

~ ~ ~

As a frequent commuter on Interstate highways, I've been in dangerous situations (hours of icy, one lane, bumper-to-bumper driving) but have never felt alone because my invisible passenger, Commute Pal, is along for the ride. Plus, I can stay alert as traffic conditions change, trust in perfect help on the journey (even if that may mean delays), and then appreciate safely reaching my destination. Have you ever experienced a traffic detour or delay only to realize down the road that you avoided a multi-car pile-up or a speed trap. Or worse? By paying attention and being aware, I've learned to trust my invisible Commuter Pal co-pilot and to "go with the flow" of traffic as well as anything that might happen on the route.

Contact Pal - the potential for providing opportunities that encourage and attract perfect connections.

Ever wished for a "magnetic personality," one that attracts others to you? When an extra boost of assurance and confidence is needed, call on this assistant to help bring perfect and positive individuals and circumstances to your attention.

~ ~ ~

I was visiting my mother at her retirement home recently, and stopped by the resident business center to answer email. I couldn't help noticing the person next to me who was compiling an application letter from written notes on the desk between us. After introducing myself, I learned that she was also a resident's daughter, and that she was applying for a computer expert job in Washington, D.C. I also sensed that she was authentic, kind, and competent. Just the person I needed for a computer project! Not only did I know her parents, but she lived nearby, she was experienced, and she was interested in helping me. I had never seen her visiting before, so I didn't think it was a random meeting. Thanks, Contact Pal.

Dream Pal - may help in not only accessing your unconscious sleep state but in consciously remembering dream details in the morning.

Call on this staffer for divine and personally helpful dreaming states (REM stages, etc.) as well as the ability to remember any nightly information as your head hits the pillow.

Errand Pal - useful with any type of day planner device or list.

Can't fit everything into your day? I've learned to trust not only the unlimited memory but the perfect scheduling of the cosmos as I work through a long "must do" list and discover that most (and usually all) of the errands can get done. For optimum help, bring in Time Efficiency and Memory Pals to form a powerful trio!

Healthy Eating Pal - the inner voice reminding us that we are what we eat and to avoid being "fast, easy, and cheap."

How are you feeling? If "sluggish," "low energy," and "stressed" describe yourself, consider asking that only foods providing vitamins, stamina, energy, and a healthy glow come to your attention. Also request help in avoiding "empty calorie" sugary, fatty, and salty fast foods. Ask for help when feeling especially hungry and during grocery shopping. Combine with Coach if your goal is to gain a more conscious control over food choices (fresh or freshly prepared) and appetites (stopping when satisfied, for instance).

Human Resources Pal - a personal source for suggesting specialized staff to your Cosmic Office Inc.

Individuals and their circumstances change, and this helper may propose various "cosmic consultants" to specifically assist you in any endeavor, however large or small. Just ask!

Idea Pal - eases the pressure to come up with something new and different when stuck in a rut.

Depending on your preferences (working independently or from an office desk/cubicle) or personal aspects (left- or right-brained), it's possible to call on Idea Pal—trusting that a brainstorm will come along in the perfect place (the shower?) at the perfect time. Consider combining with:

Inspiration Pal - focused, less general assistance toward a specific goal.

What a team within your Cosmic Office! Idea Pal, Inspiration Pal, and Intuition Pal! Ask to be inspired, let go of any presumptions; and be aware of various symbols, signals, clues, or casual conversations that may crop up.

~ ~ ~

It's amazing and especially entertaining to be in the flow and receiving "Ah-ha!" moments. Back in 1986, I was interested in using (brand new) desktop publishing, but didn't know what to write about or how to justify buying a personal Macintosh computer. Driving home from work (and when least expecting it), inspiration hit me. The idea came fully formed, and it matched my interests, capabilities, values, and connections. *Senior Activity Ideas* was born on that afternoon. The "inspired" bi-monthly newsletter provided information for people serving aging adults. It provided me with invaluable personal experience in writing, editing, publishing; plus a job guarantee twenty-six years later. (And I was able to buy that Macintosh!)

Intuition Pal - may be called on during efforts to reconnect with one's "gut feelings" and insights.

Intuition is "a natural ability or power that makes it

possible to know something without any proof or evidence." (Merriam-Webster.com) This sixth sense is a gift or present we are born with, and it might be the presence that keeps on giving—as long as we remember to rely, apply, and gratify.

Inventory Pal - assistance for taking stock of your life.

What's going on with you, goal-wise? Where are you now (friends, family, career, fun, finances, resources, responsibilities, etc.), where are you going, and how are you going to get there? Call on Inventory Pal for reminders to pause, contemplate, assess, and plan.

Locator Pal - help in finding what's been misplaced.

Have you ever put something in a "safe place that I won't forget" and then—forget where? Call on Locator Pal to help locate that safe place, but realize that time ("I need it now!") and importance is irrelevant when relying on helpers from the universe or cosmos. Instead, keep calm and trust that when (and how) requested results appear may be out of anybody's immediate control. Step back, relax, and be assured that the moment of assistance will be perfect (and possibly surprising).

~ ~ ~

I've called on my Locator Pal to help me find valuables and money that I stashed away years ago, and then I relax and sometimes forget that I've even asked for help. While daydreaming at my desk one day, an old folder on a bookshelf caught my eye. Inside was a bank envelope with cash I had put away in a "safe place" three years earlier.

Has this ever happened to you?

~ ~ ~

One afternoon I noticed I was missing an earring (why didn't someone tell me?), and it could have been anywhere within a 30-mile radius. I figured it was long gone, but mentally turned its recovery over to Locator Pal. About a year later, I was digging up a plant and saw a glint of gold in the third shovelful of dirt. It was my missing earring with a broken hinge clasp! Flabbergasted, I gave thanks to Locator Pal and trusted even more in what's possible "with a little help from my friends."

Lunch Pal - may be the perfect lunch date!

The mid-day meal can be a pleasant, nourishing experience when partnering with your invisible "Lunch Pal." Do the work by planning to pack a less expensive meal, connect with friends/coworkers, or suggest a restaurant. Then take it easy and rely on your imaginary helper to provide the perfect seat (no waiting!), menu choices, and conversation. Your mood may improve, and there is always the possibility of returning to work more relaxed and ready for clearer thinking and higher productivity.

Manager Pal - helps round up the team members.

With an ever-widening and expanding circle of helpers, create another position that keeps track of individual (imaginary) assistants. Manager pal also requires your purposeful attention, and with consistent and regular contact can become a reliable "go to" helper.

~ ~ ~

While writing, I can imagine individual helpers (Author Pal, Editor Pal, Thesaurus Pal, Coach, Word

Processing/Computer Pal, and Organizing Pal) all on track and helping me in perfect ways. I can imagine a manager for my own "Cosmic Writing Office." What would be best for you?

Memory Pal - additional memory help for use anywhere, any time!
Provide this helper with what you wish to remember; then relax and be ready to receive the information.

~ ~ ~

Memory Pal was the first staff member I created for my Cosmic Office, and this helper is called on all day and in the middle of the night (the staff never sleeps!). I get jolted awake with thoughts such as "must not forget" or "what a great idea." In the past, I would lie awake repeating the reminder to myself—getting more and more agitated as time ticked away. I might have to remember something required for work, an item for the shopping list, or something to do (charge the phone, change the thermostat, run an errand, etc.). Now I repeat each "memo to self," visualize the word or activity, and turn the reminder over to my personal "Memory Pal" with confidence that a mental reminder will, indeed, pop into my head just when I need it. Then I easily drift back to sleep. If something is especially critical, I find myself being prompted to write a reminder note or even put something by the front door so I can't possibly miss it in the morning rush.

Motivator Pal - a little voice that helps me get past the 10AM, 3PM, and 9PM "gotta have a (salty or sugary) snack" prime times and to consider healthy cold veggies instead.

What's your preference? Depend on Coach Pal exclusively, or combine with your "motivator." Try calling on the Coach for long-term, on-going assistance toward a goal—with Motivator Pal for immediate help.

Navigation Pal - one of the many travel experts I use on the road and off.

Rely on Traffic Pal, Parking Pal, and even Commute Pal, and any road anxiety may be relieved as "Team Travel" invisibly assists. Accomplish any necessary preparation by knowing the route, maintaining the auto (or bicycle), departing with time to spare—all while anticipating safe, efficient travel as the cosmic helpers ride along and guide the way through your own intuitive direction.

~ ~ ~

As someone who has driven many miles in all types of traffic and road conditions, I realize how scary a collision happening four cars ahead or a sudden lane closure or detour can be. There are choices: we can react too quickly, take time to think of options, or take a deep breath and relax for a split second while intuition helps out. In an unfamiliar and congested area, do I take the upcoming, unknown exit to avoid a potential accident? If faced with two road choices to the same destination, which do I choose? I always ask myself (Cosmic Office staff) to provide guidance, and the answer comes to me. Regular and consistent use and trust of the "Cosmic GPS" Navigation Pal may transform directionality in all of us—even those who admit to having no sense of direction.

Parking Pal - assistance in locating parking spaces.

Many people routinely visualize the "perfect parking space" (conveniently located, roomy, legal, and available for an extended length of time), so these helpers must be busy! It's uncanny how frequently a space opens up in the most congested and popular places—especially if the driver is relaxed, watchful, trusting in assistance, and not in a hurry (most "Pals," being in the no-time realm, don't like being rushed). Stories are legendary about parking at a new age store in California. The majority of customers knew how to manifest spaces so often that finding an available spot was a challenge for all.

~ ~ ~

One summer day I had to drive into Washington, D.C. for a midday appointment in Georgetown, an area with narrow streets and parking restrictions. Even allowing for traffic, I was surprised by the easy trip into town. I asked my Parking Pal for help, turned onto a random street, and noticed one open space— perfect in every way. It was in the shade, free for two hours, and less than 20 feet from my appointment! Plus, I didn't have to parallel park and had an extra hour to have coffee at a Starbucks located half a block away. The entire scenario was hard to believe, but true.

~ ~ ~

Just today, I was meeting a friend for lunch. Hoping my Parking Pal would find the perfect (free) location, I was happy to see a large space, but it was a bit further away than expected (I forgot to add "nearby" to the request). That was okay. I easily fit into the parking spot and began walking—only to see another open space I could have used that was two blocks closer to the restaurant. In seconds, it was taken; and then I understood the reason for being attracted (directed) to the original space. I relaxed, looked around, and saw leaf colors of red and gold against a brilliant blue sky. The extra walking distance provided me with a chance to appreciate the seasonal colors that I would have missed with the second, more convenient, spot.

Project Pal - help in keeping one or more efforts on task and moving toward completion.

Who doesn't have a project? Or several? From personal (daily blog or journal writing, painting a room) to professional (selling products), any progress can be slowed down by a wide variety of setbacks, distractions, or even excuses. Call on this Pal and ask for reminders (nudges, etc.) so you can regularly take steps toward completion. Bring in helping reinforcements such as Motivator Pal, Time Efficiency Pal, and Coach for even more powerful assistance in finishing the job.

Public Speaking Pal - shares the podium while providing support and encouragement during stressful times.

There are those who enjoy speaking in public, those who can easily create and memorize a captivating speech, those who can extemporize at a moment's notice, and those who are naturally witty. I am none of these people, so speaking of any kind brings anxiety with corresponding sweat and momentary amnesia.

When faced with a speaking event, request help from Public Speaking Pal in writing, rehearsing, and presenting; and possibly discover greater inner confidence as well as support for success.

~ ~ ~

I was looking forward to the weekend one Friday when an email arrived with news of dread: in two days I would have to talk for twenty minutes from a church pulpit to a congregation accustomed to hearing excellent speakers. With little time to prepare either the script or my nerves, I called on my Public Speaking Pal for help in relaxing and in finding the right words. On Sunday morning, I asked again for help with notes, to keep my hands from shaking, and for speaking coherently and clearly—even up to the balcony seats. It was definitely a relief when the message seemed to be well received, and I gave Public Speaking Pal lots of applause.

Receptionist Pal or Greeter Pal - may welcome or even attract contacts that could assist in social or career goals.

Working in combination with Contact Pal, imagine that your Cosmic Office Inc. team members have the potential to "greet" or to bring to your attention a variety of human helpers just by asking, getting out, and tuning in to seemingly random conversations and information.

~ ~ ~

Having a unified, everyone-on-the-same-page staff can make dreams come true because focus plus vision (plus personally-created/imagined energetic help) can provide unbelievable results.

I knew that a group of personal helpers could be created in my imagination (Step 1) when I decided (Step 3) that going on a cruise to warm-water ports in February would be especially wonderful. Yes! It seemed like a great idea, but there were big no's in real life: no money and no time off. But, it didn't cost anything to imagine swimming and snorkeling in warm salt water on both my birthday and Valentines Day, so I imagined—a lot! And sure enough, through an amazing mix of helping circumstances (Steps 5 and 6) I went on a cruise the next winter! That was fifteen years ago, and somehow (by paying attention to helpful invisible friends and appreciating their powers —Step 7) events happen that put me somewhere in the Caribbean every February!

Reference Pal - may help provide not only a query but its response.

What's the question? What's the answer? Where can I locate additional information? Where do I start? From a calm or meditative state, ask for help in formulating the question or request, and then be aware of incoming informational clues not only from conversations and nature, but during seemingly random Internet searching and bookstore or library browsing.

Security Pal - possible safety from another dimension.

Believe it or not, through the ages people have visualized or conjured up energetic power expansion of their physical bodies with personal electromagnetic space. This "energy field," according to Caroline Myss, may extend "...as far out as your outstretched arms and the full length of your body."[32] Others suggest a more expansive life-force plus various techniques for discovering, utilizing, and maintaining energy protection. In a non-fearful frame of mind, try calling on what you believe is "the force" (God, prayer, cosmic bliss, spirit, divine power, etc.). Imagine being surrounded by personal power in the form of pure loving goodness or white energy (the combined colors of all light frequencies). This luminous power then radiates outward into a cocoon or bubble shape around your visible physical body.

~ ~ ~

In addition to regular use and appreciation of my own white light energy, I frequently "amp it up" and modify the size of the cocoon shape to accommodate various situations. For instance, in a crowd of jostling people I take a deep breath, imagining positive white protective rays and breathe out—expanding my energy field to create comfortable space between myself and others. The same technique of expanding out a white light energy "bumper" around a car can be used to possibly provide protective space and to prevent impacts from traffic and deer.

Sleep Pal - extra assistance in relaxing before and during sleep.

Before bedtime, call on Sleep Pal for assistance in soothing, restful, rejuvenating slumber. Let go of any distractions or worries temporarily and expect serenity during the night. Add Dream Pal for a healthy sleep time combination.

Time Efficiency Pal - extra help during over-scheduling.

Can you say no? If not, call on Time Efficiency Pal to assist with to-do lists or agendas gone wild.

~ ~ ~

I was suddenly awakened at 3AM with the uncomfortable realization that everything I had scheduled or promised to do that morning was probably impossible to accomplish. Already anxious, the mental itemizing and juggling kept me wide awake until I calmed down with some deep breathing and connected with my Time Efficiency Pal. Assistance for perfect functioning and successful achievement of the day's tasks was requested, and I went back to sleep—trusting that the day would unfold according to a plan beyond what could possibly be imagined. All I had to do was stay focused, do my best, and quit wasting any extra energy with worry.

Five hours later, I awoke to the sound of rain (not predicted) and instantly knew there was now a perfect reason for not doing item #1 on my to-do list (delivering an enormous hand-painted paper banner that couldn't get wet). Suddenly three and half hours opened as a result of the steady rain—just enough time to do everything else on the list, plus more time to improve the banner art before final (dry) delivery the next day.

~ ~ ~

Another example of assistance from Time Efficiency Pal: I was trying to relax enough to sleep, but my brain was busy wondering how I could possibly add a twenty minute cardio workout plus stretch and strength training to my already overloaded daily schedule. I connected with my Cosmic Office staff—specifically Time Efficiency Pal—and asked for help. In the early morning I heard three rings from nearby wind chimes and simultaneously received a thought that the chimes were a clue. That is, I would be gently awakened earlier each day in a lovely way and in time for exercising.

Time Efficiency Pal has become a reliable imaginary friend for matching the to-do list to the time available. Trusting this helper and staying focused and relaxed with each immediate task provides me with efficiency beyond belief. Somehow, situations change, traffic jams clear, appointments are canceled, and green lights prevail.

Travel Pal - assistance during excursions near and far.

Is travel becoming too complicated and uncomfortable for you? Set up an itinerary, get to the airport/train/port on time, ask for help on the journey, and never leave home without an invisible Travel Pal. Many things can go wrong, yet how many things can go right and to my advantage is amazing to me. I've brought my cosmic team along during travels around the world, and there's never any whining, seasickness, nor jet lag.

~ ~ ~

A recent example of Travel Pal help illustrates how asking for the perfect solution (with unlimited possibilities), doing the work necessary, and being aware of opportunities might create almost unbelievable events. It's as if divine universal energy is stretching my sense of what could be possible in a delightful and imaginative way.

My husband and I took advantage of an extraordinary travel sale that we "happened" to see online. The offer included a flight from Dulles International Airport (outside Washington, D.C.), transfers by bus from the Newark, New Jersey, destination to the pier in New York City, a 7-day Princess cruise (including all food, lodging, entertainment) to Southampton, England, a bus ride to Heathrow Airport, and a return flight back to Dulles for not much more than $450.00 each.

We drove to the Dulles area before the flight and located a used book store "out of the blue." While my husband browsed and bought books, I found a drug store nearby and looked through magazines for beaders and beading. I noticed an article featuring award-winning examples of the craft and learned that the national prize winning creations were currently on display at a museum in New York City. Although unfamiliar with the museum, I made a mental note of the name and location and thought, "Gee, I'd really love to see this exhibit, but there won't be time to get there after landing, catching the bus, registering at the pier, and going aboard the ship." Any notion of actually attending the exhibit was so outrageous that I just let it go.

But maybe my Travel Pal had other plans, because after landing in Newark, someone said, "Haven't you heard? The ship's delayed."

"You've got to be kidding!" I thought, all the while staying relaxed and trusting in the perfect circumstances—the flight landed safely and on time, after all.

Our cruise colleague continued: "There was a bad storm on the trip north. The furniture and anything that wasn't tied down was tossed all over. The Captain decided to slow the boat and avoid even worse weather. There's a 24-hour delay."

"Wow! That almost never happens!" I said, still not realizing the extent of the (divinely modified) travel plans for us.

"Right!" continued the "in the know" traveler, "And the late arriving cruise passengers who had other plans for return flights aren't very happy about the delay."

For a brief second, I had a very human reaction: "Sheesh! This is a big inconvenience!" But then I calmed down (travel is an adventure, after all), trusted that the cruise line would take care of us, and that the trip would be perfect in every way. Plus, there was nothing we could do at the moment, other than get in line and wait—wait for the transfer bus, for news, for directions.

So we relaxed, got on the bus, got off at the pier in Manhattan, and waited some more. Eventually, we learned that all of us 2,000 passengers would be staying overnight in New York City—courtesy of Princess Cruise Lines—and that we would be taken directly to our hotels. Then we would be picked up the next day, bussed back to the pier when the ship was due to finally arrive, and then depart for Southampton, England.

Princess booked us into a recently renovated Sheraton Hotel with lovely new carpeting, furnishings, and top-quality pillows and linens. According to the rate card on the back of the door, the charge was well over $200.00 per night that we didn't have to pay.

But the adventure was just beginning, so we decided to "trust and relax and let go and enjoy" with a generous meal voucher and free time in the Big Apple.

The next day dawned as perfect as the first sunny and warm day in spring can be—so sublime and welcome that almost everyone we met was smiling. What a gift! To find ourselves unexpectedly in New

York City and free to do whatever we wanted until late afternoon. I located the museum with beading prize winners mentioned in the magazine and found it on the same side of the street and less than four doors away from our hotel! Plus, the attendance fee was reduced for that day. After viewing the exhibit, I walked a few blocks to Bloomingdale's and found my husband's favorite brand of shirts on sale for 50% off!

Later, we reclaimed our bags at the hotel, hopped onto the chartered bus, checked in at the pier, and began our cruise with a sunset "sail-by" the Statue of Liberty. In addition to all the serendipitous "gifts" of experiences, location, value, convenience, and good luck, we were each refunded about $200.00 for the day we "lost" on the cruise (but gained in New York City).

Writer Pal - help with expressing thoughts for yourself and others.

Everyone writes something, even if it's on a smart phone, paper, or computer. If you hope to write clear and clever prose, consider inviting Writer Pal as a personal "ghost writer," and imagine extra help with whatever has to be communicated.

~ ~ ~

At this very moment (and during the manuscript process), I'm appreciating all the instant help or ongoing assistance in every way. My Writer Pal can't be seen or heard, but when a thought or word comes to mind "out of the blue," I have to smile, type it up, and be thankful for the extra assistance. In addition to Writer Pal, I also rely on Thesaurus Pal, Spelling Pal, Editing Pal, and others, and "we" celebrate at the finish of each chapter.

Disclaimer and Staffing Note:
Non-physical staff members are not created and never available to take the place of actual (physical) hands-on and legally required and professional representation and advice. As creator and manager of any assistance, "due diligence" is required. That is, you must do the physical work—in addition to locating reputable, recommended, and experienced experts who may be needed and necessary to help you complete or accomplish any required physical or mental tasks.

Do you have a more complicated life or a tendency to micromanage? Do you require specialists in certain areas of work? For the ultimate Cosmic Office Inc., create a comprehensive staff and even an office manager to personally assist. Then share your ideas and your names for personal helpers with others.

My staff is created. Now what?

It's time to get acquainted with your staff by working together on one or more chores or assignments. After following the 7 Speedy Steps and creating your personal Cosmic Office, ask a staff member for assistance. Keep the request simple and in harmony with what you can do to support the helper. For example, asking your own Time Efficiency Pal for invisible help during the day is useful as long as you, the manager of your staff, stay focused and accomplish what needs to be done—trusting that perfect assistance will occur at the perfect time. The process is one of teamwork between your own work in the physical world and your personal helpers in the unlimited, invisible cosmos.

As soon as connections or requests are made, help begins—whether it's obvious or not. By being focused and doing your part, it's even possible that any ongoing assistance might not result in a recognizable, clear, logical outcome. This is normal. The more you and your invisible assistants work together, the easier it will be to recognize clues, signs, inspirations, and other evidence of help. Early on, situations and "Ah-has" might be considered coincidental, but the results can be perfectly timed and far beyond our human imaginations.

While getting acquainted with the capabilities and talents of each helper, remain positive—trusting that the outcome (however expected or unexpected) will be perfect for you. Also become familiar with newly imagined staff members by calling on them frequently for help or just to say "Hi."

Faithfully do your work, be aware, and expect the unexpected! Intentionally directing and trusting a positively created personal helper may result in astonishing outcomes. I am often surprised with the unbelievable results that occur with perfect timing. I hear myself saying, "Oh, wow!" and then "Thank you!" to daily examples of help.

Of the "7 Speedy Steps," the seventh is the easiest. In addition to thanking each invisible helper for any assistance, try to stay grateful at all times. Why? One never knows when help might be continuing "behind the scenes." Since creating a staff and working in cooperation with helpers for many years, I seem to automatically remain in an "attitude of gratitude" for any past, ongoing, and future assistance.

When asked how I accomplish so much during the twenty-four hour day, I explain the 7 Speedy Steps

Process and give credit to my personal Cosmic Office Inc. team members.

Currently helping me are:

Motivation Pal

Relaxation Pal

Writing Pal

Oprah Winfrey connection Pal

Inspiration Pal

Idea Pal

Time Efficiency Pal

Coach

Healthy Eating Pal

Memory Pal...

and many more.

Reminders

Invisible cosmic helpers are always nearby, and seem to like being contacted with courtesy, kindness, and clear, focused intention and trust. Try to be patient while your work is ongoing, yet expect perfect outcomes—whatever they may be. Trust that your decision to imagine helpers instantly creates personal connections of unlimited energy and that perfect assistance will arrive at the perfect moment and in a possibly personal way.

Trying to "second guess," or adding presumptions or ideas for expectations is a normal reaction, but try to let your staff helpers do what they can in the background. That way, you won't "...disturb your guides' natural warmth and good intentions."[33]

While staff is helping with a task or solution, you are also working and doing whatever is necessary and possible in daily life. There's no "free lunch." It's a collaboration of faithful imaginary helpers created from your own personal energy. A partnership implies that everyone involved is focused on the necessary tasks as well as outcomes. Staff may provide assistance, but as creator and manager of the staff, you are responsible for all choices or decisions. That includes deciding to ask for help (Step 3), intentionally creating a helper (Step 4), taking personal action (Step 5), being aware (Step 6), and appreciating any outcome (Step 7). In other words, your team of assistants "...cannot and will not live your life for you."[34]

~ ~ ~

In 2003, an idea came to me: design a woman's undergarment out of a fabric that could "wick" away the perspiration of the wearer. The thought was there, but nothing else. I put together my cosmic staff "experts," asked for help, and received clues that directed me to friends with a fabric store.

Since procrastination is a favorite hobby of mine, the entire process could have stopped there, but I wanted to honor the creative (maybe divine) source of the idea and started with a "to do" list. I followed steps on the list, made calls, kept appointments, had three personal fittings, created prototypes, and spent hours researching fabrics.

In the process, help arrived in almost weird, unexpected ways—even in one of those free Sunday newspaper inserts that advertised undergarments. Rather than recycling it with the rest of the paper, I called the 800 number—fully expecting a recorded message and menu of options. Instead, the call was answered immediately and I was connected with someone who was not only helpful, but who happened to have an encyclopedic knowledge of the products. When asked if there was something like my garment idea for sale, she replied "No." We kept talking, and she said that my "U*B [Sweat Free Under Breast Bra Skirt] Soft Sip Slimmer" could be a new and useful additional product. Then she gave me suggestions and mentioned her location: less than ten miles from my in-law's house in Ohio. And I could meet with her. Imagine!

The special connections continued at the local university library where I researched what colors would best apply to the packaging and what names would be perfect for the garment. Then I created a prototype—complete with label and packaging.

In the meantime, a clue appeared in my mailbox "out of the blue" in the form of an invitation to a special event for a new library opening. I sent an RSVP and went to the program and then to the lunch afterwards. The person next to me in the buffet line worked at the university library and started a conversation. Was I a librarian? And if so, where? When learning that it wasn't at a library, she asked what I was doing, so I took a deep breath and explained the undergarment project to this perfect stranger.

"Oh," she said, "You need to get with _____. He's a big manufacturer using those kinds of [wicking] fabrics, and he lives nearby."

That seemed to be an incredible bit of helpful information, so I thought, "Why not?"

It was easy to locate the name and residence in the phone book, so I called and had a conversation with this busy international manufacturer! He was curious: how did I get his number? I mentioned the librarian's information referral, and he agreed to meet for coffee.

Then I went into high gear, perfecting the garment sample (with ironed-on labeling and fabric contents), creating an online presentation, and memorizing a short sales pitch. A few coffee dates and many questions ("How did you do all this?") later, he proposed a product manufacturing plan.

I sincerely believe that my **Cosmic Office Inc.** staff was helping with amazing assistance and answers during this entire six-month process, and I followed intuitive prompts with the best work I could do. At this moment (over ten years later), I would love to report that I'm selling on television, own a popular online store, and have to decide which vacation home to visit next week. Unfortunately, I don't find myself in that situation. That's another story for another time.

But I like to learn from my success and failures, and in reviewing the entire scenario, maybe I forgot (or wasn't ready and mentally equipped) to consider vital components in getting final results and sales. Maybe I expected too much of the manufacturer. Maybe the timing for production was off. Maybe I will never learn the full story. But I am sure of one thing: the process was a huge learning experience and did provide me with some results—a wealth of information and confidence.

I learned something else from this experience (and many others): that my expectations were ridiculously simple and ordinary. Apparently, overwhelmingly fantastic possibilities and help are available with staff assistance. By personally asking and intending, help may arrive in unexpected, amazing, and amusing ways. But the process seems to be individualized and special.

I have experienced information and solutions that seem to be a long way beyond the bounds of possibility. Maybe they are! But regardless of any incredible results, the responsibility of deliberately cooperating with staff helpers and choosing what actions to take are completely personal and require using "...your own judgment."[35] All of us have the freedom and ability to choose what to ask, what to do, and how to respond in all situations.

Want some ideas on what your staff can do for you? Continue reading and learn how to incorporate imaginary helpers in daily living. Join in our Cosmic Office Inc. blog conversations at
    www.CosmicOfficeInc.com

"Life is not measured by the number of breaths we take, but by the moments that take our breath away."

-- anonymous

4 MANAGE YOUR COSMIC OFFICE INC.

Blend Helpers into your life

Classic business and organization models often feature a "hierarchical" or pyramid-shaped diagram with the big boss or leader at the top and workers in levels below. There's an idea that supporting staff workers of a company (or voters in a government) belong at the very top; but typically the Chief Executive Officer (CEO) or (managing) Director (of the Board of Directors) holds the most power in an organization and is positioned at the apex of the pyramid.

A diagram with power located at the top[36] also may not indicate relationships among and between managerial levels—other than suggesting a "top down" or "trickle down" pattern.

Another organizational option lists staff positions set up along a horizontal plane. These supervisory managers may have more responsibility in making decisions within their specific capacity. But in most organizational charts, obligations to consumers and their roles in the general scheme of things aren't always clearly indicated.

Since your Cosmic Office Inc. is conceived by you and for your specific needs and desires, you're in the position of making decisions for yourself. In other words, imagine yourself (self-promoted to CEO!) as the "hub" of a burst pattern, or type of "organigraph," as proposed by Mintzberg and Van der Heyden in "...How Companies Really Work."[37] In this scenario, you are the source of energy at the center of your organization and providing direction to your staff. That direction includes both frequent and clear communications, plus trust that your incorporated office staff will supply the perfect outcome at the perfect time.

Any personal office is a personal invention providing for your needs and desires and it can be organized in any number of ways. I envision my helping staff set up in a kind of hub pattern, with lines ending in tiny "explosion" patterns. That is, the lines extending from myself (the center) illustrate rays of energy connections to and from each helper. These lines are of varying lengths because at any moment each staff member may be assisting on a long or a short term request. At the outer ends of each line are shorter rays resembling "bursts." Looking like fireworks, these rays represent not only the unlimited abilities of each helper, but how requests can connect with the unseen universe of unlimited energy and potential

Try placing yourself in the hub center (of a wheel, for instance) surrounded by "spokes" or lines from the center of the hub (you) that each connect with a helper. In this layout, you (as the living, breathing person) are the dynamo that helps drive imaginary staff members toward cooperative goals. What's energizing the dynamo? Picture a power strip that connects your self, through your own belief and personal expression, to the source of all (unlimited, infinite universal life force, God, Divine Being, Lord, Almighty, etc.).

Blending new help into daily life

Managing a Cosmic Office of your own provides an easy opportunity to be the boss. Are you a hands-on or a relaxed type of personality? In your office, you set the rules, the number of required meetings, even the dress code! Imagine the fantasy management style of the future—with yourself in charge—and with an organized team assisting with your own personal mission and vision.

Real life working or supervising backgrounds in typical business offices doesn't matter here. Experience with one, two, ten, or many more personnel isn't important or required. It doesn't even matter if previous working experience has been in a clinic, office, home, retail store, school, or hospital. What matters is that your Cosmic Office is personally created with your imagination, individual ideas, purposes, and goals—all to benefit yourself!

What type of organization would be best? You are creating staff members and setting personal agendas that may frequently change according to need, so being flexible is key. By imagining or "hiring" personal helpers, whatever you decide and whatever you choose is always possible. Once a staff has been imagined or invented, one way of remembering helpers is to keep a list of daily or long-term objectives and names of helpers who could be called on for assistance in those objectives.

For anyone who prefers to micromanage, consider imagining a Board of Directors or a Board of Advisors—complete with agendas, regularly scheduled meetings, and recommended actions directed toward your personal goals. In either case, your task as Board Chairperson is to ask for help as needed—all the while acting in partnership with helpers to accomplish whatever is required to meet your aims and purpose.

Not certain of anything? Ask for assistance. Since the Cosmic Office has been created in and of your identity and imagination, the staff is already aware of what you're thinking and planning on another (unseen) level of consciousness. This suggestion is designed to help you begin to connect with "no-time" cosmic energy while you stay focused in the present. Depending upon what's asked of them, it's possible that invisible helpers could keep your vision steady and provide not only answers and replies, but intuitive guidance and advice regarding your progress and accomplishments.

The basics: AM

Greet staff. Review your plans for the day. What do you expect to accomplish by yourself? In addition to typical chores (emails, phone messages, etc.), will you need a parking space, help with travel or traffic, concentrating on an assignment or workout, bringing a project toward completion, or managing time to accomplish everything? Or something else?

As with any new job hire—anywhere—there's usually a period of adjustment and accommodation of staff personnel. The same situation may occur with your Cosmic Office. Remember to stay calm and steady in the belief that helpers are always near.

Throughout the day, the most important tasks may be: connecting with imagined staff members by asking for help and support, accomplishing any physical work required for the task at hand, and tuning in to any incoming answers and other clues that your staff is working...for you! In other words, trusting that circumstances beyond your control will benefit you in perfect (but not necessarily expected) ways.

During any day (and depending upon your management style), gather helpers together in a staff meeting, and:

Enjoy the moment with staff. Then, direct each helper to tasks (specific or general) that would be of benefit to the total collaborative effort (you and your Cosmic Office together).

Acknowledge staff members who have been "hired" for special expertise or who may be tasked with an ongoing project.

Remember that any personal participation and anticipation remains in the action of what may be occurring (not in any immediate or predetermined results). Be open to possibility and maybe even surprise.

In the state of cooperation with your helpers, do what you can while being mindful of the perfect assistance and solutions that are already "in the works."

Create helpers as necessary—always providing a name and introducing them to the existing staff.

An excellent way to manage personally-created assistants is to check in with your own Cosmic Office on a daily basis—adjusting any of your staff requests and monitoring your own progress in meeting personal goals. Help (tasks, ideas, "coincidences," etc.) can arrive almost immediately (as in Ah-ha!" moments) or occur over several seconds, minutes, hours, days, weeks, or months. Regardless of the time frame, interactions between yourself and the helpers you imagine are completely personal relationships. What would be best? Being with a group of helpers, being in a partnership, or working with an interdependent, family-type organization?

The Basics: PM

Review or recall individual events or activities during the day that were possibly assisted by specific staff members (no task is too small to take for granted). Plan for your evening cooperation and comfort with social, sleep, relaxation, and dream staff. Before bedtime, give thanks and appreciation not only for the help received but for any ongoing staff possibilities of support.

Working together

Most family units (including your "family" of Cosmic Office assistants) benefit from regularly organized casual meetings for discussions regarding changes in schedules or changes based on new information.

My family sat down together for most evening meals, and the topics of conversation typically ranged from what happened at school to what might happen on the weekend. Often loud and argumentative, we kids were still expected to be courteous to each other and to pay attention and listen when my parents spoke. They were definitely in charge, and this "top-down" authority style continued with "family council" sessions that everyone had to attend. I clearly remember my father calling all of us five active children "to sit down and be quiet" around the dining room table in a "just for family" meeting.

The anticipation of one of these scheduled sessions was especially stressful, as we kids didn't know the agenda and (as less-than-perfectly-behaved children) imagined the worst. Really important news involving the entire family was announced then, such as a new job, a new location, a new car, or a new budget; with decisions already seriously considered and decided by our parents (the managers at the top). Occasionally, our opinions were taken into consideration, but not until we were older (and less inclined to pay attention or to listen).

A more equitable and generous process of sharing information is described by Bruce Feiler. In his "Family Inc." article in *The Wall Street Journal*,[38] he mentions establishing a 'weekly family meeting' and adopting the "agile development" management concept by organizing members of the family (staff) into small teams, convening daily progress sessions, and scheduling weekly reviews. These meetings have led to increased communication, improved productivity, and lower stress—with everyone having a voice and each family member involved in taking responsibility.

What type of regular team contact would work best for you?

The possibilities are endless! Imaginatively create a Board of Directors for your own Cosmic Office and share responsibilities with trusted helpers who are also Directors (or consulting managers) for the organization named You. As long as your method of organizing feels comfortable and works for you, do it! Since you're in charge, you can always change, or "tweak," what will work for your personal life and lifestyle.

Regularly asking for help with new tasks may mean creating additional staff. It's also possible to imagine a helper specifically assigned to remind you of the path you've already chosen and the goals you are working toward. Life can be complicated and challenging, and sometimes knowing that help is available in all ways, always, is a tremendous comfort.

Whenever invisible staff members are chosen, trusted, organized, and appreciated, it's conceivable that interactions between yourself and each helper will probably be similar to the relationship between yourself and any dependable friend on earth. That is, check in frequently and recognize your helpers without getting involved in their work. Converse with your staff silently or out loud. Stay in contact. Write thank you notes (everyone likes to feel connected and appreciated) and be consistently sincere—believing in the power of other unseen or invisible energies that are available to assist you in many ways.

These helping energies may become more and more obvious when benefits are received on a regular basis, and may enhance your personal confidence. How? By creating a trusting bond with your self and individual power (unlimited human potential).

Many positive experiences have convinced me that cosmic helpers are always available. I have learned to do the actual work—staying positive, relaxing, and accomplishing what I can—all the while absolutely trusting that individualized personal assistance will arrive at the perfect time and that all will be...perfect.

5 DIY (DO IT YOURSELF)

Personal Cosmic Office Inc. Helpers
Speedy Staffing in 7 Steps

You are the president, CEO, or producer of your show called life! Take charge and create your own Cosmic Office Inc. now!

Relax by meditating. Or, take deep breaths in and out for three minutes. New oxygen is now circulating through your body and energizing any action. Ready? Now imagine what would be immediately helpful (assistance with sleeping, remembering, time management, deciding what to cook for supper, etc.).

1. Believe that help is yours for the asking. As living (feeling, thinking) beings, anything is possible with belief, attention, and action. As a matter of course, we all receive assistance (a smile, another moment of life on earth) every day.

2. Trust that helpers have your best interests at heart. Since each helper is being created through your positive imagination, any assistance provided is the best for you.

3. Decide to ask for help. The action of making a decision tends to start something—adding a spin of extra energy to the process and streamlining any response.

4. Intentionally imagine or invent a helper. The process continues as you choose to imagine, name, and get acquainted with one or more personalized assistants.

5. Act or "do the work" possible. Since your imagined helper exists in the unlimited, non-physical realms of imagination, you must make the physical effort (work) required for the partnership to succeed.

6. Be aware of possible clues or signs of staff support. Clues could be obvious ("Ah-ha!") or subtle ("...what was that?"). Living in the present moment and enjoying your surroundings is important and a vital component of connecting with your intuitive self. (Turn off the phone now and then; smell the roses).

7. Appreciate every step in the process. Easy! Say a silent or even a really, really loud "Thank you!" It only takes a second to appreciate assistance (and assistants) and it feels good, too.

Return to Step 4 (intentionally imagine or invent a helper) and create more helpers for your immediate and long-term life needs, following through with the remaining steps or actions. Repeat as necessary.

30 Minute Staffing

Are you a "get it done now" person? Follow the 7 Speedy Steps Process and set a timer for twenty minutes. While the moments tick away, get going and make a list of what is most important in your life. This may include family, career, personal goals, hobbies, and much more.

The exercise is important because having a fixed timeframe boosts focus and can shift any left brain detail over-thinking into a more intuitional, true self (right brain) consciousness. Writing down what instinctively comes to mind in that twenty minutes also energetically "revs up" the process and your creative thinking.

When the bell rings, stop. Or, keep listing ideas and items while your thoughts flow. Ask for ideas or for help "out of the blue" in finishing your list and keep writing. Then, take a deep breath, congratulate yourself, and give thanks to the invisible, yet powerful, inspiration of the universe.

The list can be used as a blueprint, or template, of where you are now, where you want to be, and how far you could go in your life. Next, consider what is personally important and put a star next to each item that is absolutely vital to your mental and physical wellbeing.

Then go back to the starred items and for each one invent a helper who could be of service to you. Imagine a name, title, and/or responsibility for each helper, and make an appointment (promise) to be in regular contact. These frequent get-togethers can create focus for your personal vision by keeping track of any actions and progress being made toward goals and results. Since any Cosmic Office is a partnership between the "imaginer" (yourself) and the imagined (helpers), communication is important.

Would reminders of any "meetings" with your helpers be useful? Since it may feel new and different to suddenly have assistants and a personal staff

(Cosmic Office Inc.), consider creating a helper (maybe an "appointment secretary") for reminders. My "Memory Pal" helps me remember any sessions I've scheduled with my staff of imagined helpers.

No matter how many assistants are created or what their tasks may be, realize that help is always available. Making connections consistently with that help, doing the work, and being grateful establishes the power of coherence in every manageable "baby step" to your dreams and aspirations.

**"Keep your face to the sunshine
and you cannot see the shadow."**

-- Helen Keller

6 FAQ
(FREQUENTLY ASKED QUESTIONS)

Q: Is there a right or wrong way to ask for help and to communicate with my Cosmic Office staff?
A: Any asking should be genuine and trusting through personal belief and intention. If a request feels right to you, continue...

Q: How does guidance or help arrive?
A: Be aware of various "coincidences" and try to stay tuned in to the present moment. Begin to notice cues and clues from nature, words or songs that may be overheard (conversation, radio), and what might come along while you're doing the necessary work.
~~~

In my experience, help and direction tends to match, or synchronize, with each person's individual interests. In other words, if you have a passion for car racing on a large track, guidance might appear or become obvious through numbers (laps, race cars, seat numbers, pole positions) or even colors of the cars or conversations during the race. Sometimes I get clues to the answers of my questions (as well as encouragement) from words and messages on license plates or even bumper stickers!

Q: What if I simply can't believe that help is available for me?
A: Try believing in merely the possibility that help is there, that prayer is answered, and that you have access to an unlimited world of possibility. Then try creating/imagining one or two helpers, follow the 7

Speedy Steps, do the work, and see what happens. You might be surprised at your own power and results.

1. Believe that help is yours for the asking.
2. Trust that each helper has your best interests at heart.
3. Decide to ask for assistance.
4. Intentionally imagine or invent a helper.
5. Act and do the work necessary.
6. Be aware of possible clues or signs of staff support.
7. Appreciate every step in the process.

Q: I need all kinds of help and don't know where to start.
A: Begin with a basic, general request to cover anything such as: "Please provide me with perfect assistance in every way today." Or "Please help me to use my talents today." Then relax, do your best, and know that what you sincerely desire and work towards will arrive at the perfect time.

Q: When should I expect to get help?
A: When least expected! Be observant and tuned in to what may be going on around you. Also notice "unusual" sounds, sights, smells, or interactions with others. What suddenly grabs your attention? By taking the time to observe and to listen and to appreciate all the senses, clues to answers can be received. Sometimes help arrives immediately, and sometimes it comes along only after I let go of any left-brained, ego-based expectations and say: "Oh well." In other words, be patient, trust, and do any work you can.

Q: What if the assistance isn't what I expected?

A: In all cases, your own helping staff members, created by you, are assigned to provide you with the perfect results, at the perfect time, for your benefit or highest good (whatever that may be). Consider reexamining your intention (Step 4) of the 7 Speedy Steps Process and take the "I" out of the word "intention" (written in lower case letters). Sometimes what ego thinks is best can block, or override, information or any assistance coming from the helpers in your subconscious, true self.

Q: How can I keep everyone straight (remember each helper)?

A: Each helper imaginatively created in your mind is there to assist you, and remains in your memory. Consider writing down each helper's name, title, and responsibility if that would be useful. It doesn't matter if they are temporarily forgotten. After being imagined with intention, when the need arises and requests are made, helpers will be there.

Q: I heard (or thought I heard) an answer, but I'm not really sure—it was really fast and I wasn't paying attention.

A: Every type of answer isn't necessarily loud or obvious. If you believe that you could have missed something, it may be helpful to take a few minutes and ask: "What information is available for me?" Then, relax and pause in quiet reflection for any answers or replies that may arrive—immediately or sometime in the future. Or keep asking! Reconnecting with your own intuitive sense becomes easier and more automatic with practice.

~ ~ ~

I receive most of my guidance in visual ways, although when I do "hear" any thoughts, they seem to be a clue or an answer especially and personally for myself.

Q: What if I don't want the help or solution I've asked for and then received?
A: Good question! Since everything you have created with the 7 Speedy Steps Process is personal and individualized, you always have free choice to both ask and to ignore. It's completely up to you. You are in charge. According to the authors of *Companions in Spirit,* "...it's your responsibility...and use your own judgment."[39]

Q: What if I'm not absolutely sure that help is there for me?
A: Try it! By using the 7 Steps you may be surprised at your own power. Any help and results may turn disbelief into believing—plus it will boost your confidence! (Believe, Trust, Decide, Intend, Act, Be aware, Appreciate)

Q: When should I add other helpers to my staff?
A: Anytime you can use help in accomplishing tasks or saving time in your life. When I anticipate a specific project (creating a program, writing a book, making a speech), I usually organize a staff with help I think will be needed—in addition to my every day Cosmic Office Inc. group.

Q: What's the most important thing I can do for my staff?
A: Two things: trust (yourself/helpers) and thank.

Q: Can I ask for something not to happen or for no help?

A: Putting any request in the negative is not recommended. Try this: take what isn't wanted, and flip the idea into what is ("I don't want to be in an accident" to "Please provide the perfect, safe, effective, and efficient conditions during my travels"). The positive thinking and believing is important.

Q: Can I ask for help for someone else?

A: Many of us who regularly work with helpers and guides would say that you are the only person in charge of your actions (decisions, thinking, reacting, etc.), so it's best for others to also be personally responsible for their actions.

I wish you unlimited success and assistance.

Enjoy!

DISCLAIMER (FINE PRINT ENLARGED)

Although the reader may be creating and communicating with what is usually considered one's own energy and nonphysical identity, it is still important that helpers be conceived of in a positive state of mind, spirit, and body; and in the energy of love. With the position of CEO of your Cosmic Office Inc. comes responsibilities—to provide attention, trust, loyalty, and continued appreciation.

Ongoing contact and nurturing will support perfect results at the perfect time in the perfect manner while you provide the perfect assistance (work, attentiveness, personal choices) in everyday living.

Consulting with professional expertise and performing due diligence regarding legal or financial or healthful concerns is required before any assignment to your own Cosmic Office associates. All individual contact with helpers is an agreement and personal connection with source or divine energy and is not to be utilized for anyone else.

Please note: Any allusions to, or descriptions of, cosmic structures, arrangements, or other related information included in this print book "Cosmic Office Inc." or the electronic book of the same name have no relationship (implied or otherwise) with comics, weapons, tools, music/sound, or technology.

Published by Inky Endeavors

www.CosmicOfficeInc.com

Unattributed quotations are by Carol E. Cary Taylor

Copyright 2014 by Carol E. Cary Taylor

Paper back book edition ISBN: 978-0-9860828-0-1

Electronic book edition ISBN: 978-0-9960089-0-7

~ ~ ~

Did you find useful ideas for help in this book?

Yes? Write a review of "Cosmic Office Inc." at
www.Amazon.com
and join other readers who say:

"This is an excellent 'how to' manual, a highly organized system for applying and benefiting from the help which is available from sources outside yourself, regardless of what their nature may be.

While it is straightforward and easy to follow, *Cosmic Office Inc.* is so chock full of good ideas I found myself reading it with a pencil in hand. Some books are filled with fluff and filler with a few good ideas or suggestions thrown in here and there. This book is like condensed soup—add your own filler. If you take the time to incorporate these ideas and methods into your daily life, the benefits can be immense. I know this from my own experience." – R.B.

"Do you feel unworthy to work with God or Spirit? This book may change your mind. It helps you to see how working with God, Spirit can be as natural as combing your hair or brushing your teeth. It's a happy book that brings the Spiritual and the physical together to seem like ONE." – R.E.

Can a friend use some help?

Go to www.CosmicOfficeInc.com and order a copy

Interested in connecting with Carol online?

- go to www.CosmicOfficeInc.com

- connect with her blog

- sign up to receive news, information, and upcoming events

ABOUT THE AUTHOR

Carol Cary Taylor, author of *Cosmic Office Inc.* and *Senior Activity Ideas*, provides practical solutions to daily life through books, presentations, articles, design, training, and technology.

Her motley assortment of childhood interests and skills was recognized and encouraged at age 11 with the awarding of the Girl Scout "Dabbler" badge. Later, she earned degrees in teaching art (B.A.) and library/information technology (M.L.S.).

She has many years of experience teaching in grade schools and colleges and has spoken at conventions for Virginia school librarians and for professionals in aging and elder care. Publishing credits include books, book reviews, columns; and articles on creativity, careers, downsizing, skin care, teaching, and librarianship.

Carol traces her insatiable curiosity and creativity to a natural right/left brain balance that supports artistic endeavors with down-to-earth, organizational sensibilities. She is an experienced facilitator of Outreach seminars for The Monroe Institute, an international center of consciousness exploration and training.

"Knowledge is of two kinds.

We know a subject ourselves, or we know where we can find information upon it."

-- Samuel Johnson

NOTES AND RESOURCES

[1] *The New English Bible* (New York: Oxford University Press, 1970), 211.

[2] Ibid., 692.

[3] Price, John Randolph, *Angel Energy* (New York: Fawcett Columbine, 1995), 9.

[4] Associated Press. "Poll: Nearly 8 in 10 Americans believe in angels." CBSNews.com. CBS Corporation and CBS Broadcasting, Inc. Web. 23 Dec. 2011.

[5] Rosalind A. McKnight, *Soul Journeys* (Charlottesville: Hampton Roads, 2005), 120.

[6] Ralph Waldo Emerson, *Self-Reliance and Other Essays* (New York: Dover, 1993), 19.

[7] Eben Alexander, *Proof of Heaven: a Neurosurgeon's Journey into the Afterlife* (New York: Simon & Schuster Paperbacks, 2012), 156.

[8] Ibid., 161.

[9] Rosalind A. McKnight, 120.

[10] Ronald Shone, *Creative Visualization* (Wellingborough: Thorsons, 1984), 41.

[11] Richard Lawrence, *Unlock Your Psychic Powers* (NY: St. Martin's, 1993), 147.

[12] S., Wendy, "Ally McBeal: The Theme of Life" www.coffeerooms.com/ally/3998.html w3PG, 1998. Web. 7 Jan. 2014.

[13] McKnight, 74.

[14] Abraham-Hicks, *Abraham-Hicks Daily Planning Calendar and Study Group Workbook* (New York: Hay House, 1997), 161.

[15] *The New English Bible* (New York: Oxford University Press, 1970), 10.

[16] McKnight, 98-99.

[17] *The Quotable Woman* (Philadelphia: Running Press, 1991), 183.

[18] Judith Orloff, *Positive Energy* (New York: Harmony Books, 2004), 53.

[19] McKnight, 101.

[20] Hugh Rawson and Margaret Miner, *The Oxford Dictionary of American Quotations* (New York: Oxford University Press, 2006), 204.

[21] Leah Maggie Garfield and Jack Grant, *Companions in Spirit* (Berkeley, CA: Celestial Arts, 1984), 66.

[22] Ibid., 153.

[23] Zig Ziglar, "Edition#28." ziglar.com Web. Jan. 22, 2014.

[24] Shakti Gawain, *Creative Visualization* (New York: Bantam Books, 1982), 70.

[25] Deepak Chopra, *The Seven Spiritual Laws of Success* (San Rafael, CA: Amber-Allen Publishing, 1994), 78.

[26] Antoine de Saint-Exupéry, *The Little Prince* (New York: Harcourt, 1943) translation by Richard Howard, 63.

[27] Napoleon Hill, *The Law of Success* (Meriden, CT: Ralston University Press, 1928) eBooks on Internet Archive, 6.

[28] Louise L. Hay, *You Can Heal Your Life* (Santa Monica, CA: Hay House, 1984), 7.

[29] Robert A. Monroe. 2014. Monroeinstitute.org. The Monroe Institute.Web. 5 Jan. 2014.

[30] Moncure Daniel Conway, *The Writings of Thomas Paine, Volume IV. 1794-1796.* Age of Reason Chapter XIII - Comparison of Christianism With the Religious Ideas 2012. projectgutenberg.org. Web. 3 Jan. 2014.

[31] *Merriam-Webster.* Merriam-Webster.com. 2013. Merriam-Webster, Inc. Web. 20 Jan. 2014.

[32] Caroline Myss, *Anatomy of the Spirit* (NY: Three Rivers Press, 1996), 33.

[33] Garfield, 39.

[34] Ibid., 64.

[35] Ibid., 66.

[36] U.S. Office of Personnel Management, "Our People & Organization: Organizational Chart & Contacts." opm.gov. U.S. Office of Personnel Management. Web. 3 Jan. 2014.

[37] Henry Mintzberg and Ludo Van der Heyden, "Organigraphs: Drawing How Companies Really Work." harvardmacy.org. Sep.-Oct. 1999. Harvard Macy Institute. Web. 17 Nov. 2013.

[38] Bruce Feiler, "Family Inc." online.wsj.com. 10 Feb. 2013. Dow Jones & Company. Web. 11 Feb. 2013.

[39] Garfield, 74.

RESOURCES

Abraham-Hicks. *Abraham-Hicks Daily Planning Calendar and Study Group Workbook.* New York: Hay House, 1997. Print.

Alexander, Eben. *Proof of Heaven: a Neurosurgeon's Journey into the Afterlife.* New York: Simon & Schuster Paperbacks, 2012. Print.

Associated Press. "Poll: Nearly 8 in 10 Americans believe in angels." CBSNews.com. CBS Corporation and CBS Broadcasting, Inc. 23 Dec. 2011. Web. 23 Dec. 2011.

Castaneda, Carlos. *The Fire from Within.* New York: Pocket Books, 1991. Print.

Chopra, Deepak. *The Seven Spiritual Laws of Success*. San Rafael, CA: Amber-Allen Publishing, 1994. Print.

Conway, Moncure Daniel, *The Writings of Thomas Paine, Volume IV. 1794-1796*. "Age of Reason Chapter XIII - Comparison of Christianism With the Religious Ideas" 2012. projectgutenberg.org. Web. 3 Jan. 2014.

Eason, Cassandra. *10 Steps to Psychic Power*. London: Judy Piatkus, 2002. Print.

Emerson, Ralph Waldo. *Self-Reliance and Other Essays*. New York: Dover, 1993. Print.

Feiler, Bruce. "Family Inc." online.wsj.com. 10 Feb. 2013. Dow Jones & Company. Web. 11 Feb. 2013.

Garfield, Laeh Maggie, and Jack Grant. *Companions in Spirit*. Berkeley: Celestial Arts, 1984. Print.

Gawain, Shakti. *Creative Visualization*. New York: Bantam Books, 1982. Print.

Gilman, William H., ed. *Selected Writings of Ralph Waldo Emerson*. New York: Penguin Books, 1983. Print.

Hall, Judy. *Way of Psychic Protection*. London: Thorsons, 2001. Print.

Hay, Louise L. *You Can Heal Your Life*. Santa Monica, CA: Hay House, 1984. Print.

Hill, Napoleon. *The Law of Success*. Meriden, CT: Ralston University Press, 1928. archive.org. Internet Archive. Web. 22 Nov. 2013.

Lishtar. "Magic and Religion in Mesopotamia." GatewaystoBabylon.com. Gateways to Babylon. n.d. Web. 17 Nov. 2013.

McKnight, Rosalind A. *Soul Journeys*.

Charlottesville: Hampton Roads, 2005. Print.

Merriam-Webster.com. 2013. Merriam-Webster, Inc. Web. 20 Oct. 2013.

Mintzberg, Henry, and Ludo Van der Heyden. "Organigraphs: Drawing How Companies Really Work." harvardmacy.org. Sep.-Oct. 1999. Harvard Macy Institute. Web. 17 Nov. 2013.

Monroe, Robert A. Monroeinstitute.org. The Monroe Institute.Web. 5 Jan. 2014.

Myss, Caroline. *Anatomy of the Spirit.* NY: Three Rivers Press, 1996. Print.

The New English Bible. New York: Oxford University Press, 1970. Print.

Orloff, Judith. *Positive Energy.* New York: Harmony Books, 2004. Print.

Oxforddictionaries.com. Oxford University Press, 2013. Web. 23 Nov. 2013.

Petre'n, Mattias Georgson. "Trust--the key for successful delivery using agile methods." congresses.pmi.org. 2012. Project Management Institute. Web. 17 Nov. 2013.

"Poll: Nearly 8 in 10 Americans believe in angels." Associated Press. Online video clip. CBS Corporation and CBS Broadcasting, Inc. 23 Dec. 2011. www.cbsnews.com.

Price, John Randolph. *Angel Energy.* New York: Fawcett Columbine, 1995.

The Quotable Woman. Philadelphia: Running Press, 1991. Print.

Rawson, Hugh, and Margaret Miner. *The Oxford Dictionary of American Quotations.* New York: Oxford University Press, 2006. Print.

St. Clair, David. *David St. Clair's Lessons in*

Instant ESP. Englewood Cliffs: Prentice-Hall, 1978. Print.

Saint-Exupéry, Antoine. *The Little Prince*. New York: Harcourt, 1943. Print.

Shone, Ronald. *Creative Visualization*. Wellingborough: Thorsons, 1984. Print.

Ziglar, Zig. "Edition#28" ziglar.com Zig Ziglar. Web. Jan. 22, 2014.

Zimmer, Carl. "The Brain: Look Deep Into the Mind's Eye." <u>Discover Magazine</u>. March 23, 2010. Web. 12 Nov. 2013.

Zukav, Gary. *Soul Stories*. New York: Simon & Schuster, 2000. Print.

www.ingramcontent.com/pod-product-compliance
Lightning Source LLC
Chambersburg PA
CBHW071641050426
42443CB00026B/811